owya

D0913166

POETS

of
WORLD WAR I

RUPERT SMITH

Chicago, Illinois

© 2014 Heinemann Library
an imprint of Capstone Global Library, LLC
Chicago, Illinois

To contact Capstone Global Library, please
call 800-747-4992, or visit our web site
www.capstonepub.com

All rights reserved. No part of this publication
may be reproduced or transmitted in any form
or by any means, electronic or mechanical,
including photocopying, recording, taping, or
any information storage and retrieval system,
without permission in writing from the publisher.

Edited by Andrew Farrow, Adrian Vigliano,
    and Diyan Leake
Designed by Philippa Jenkins
Original illustrations © Capstone Global
    Library Ltd 2014
Picture research by Mica Brancic
Production by Helen McCreath
Originated by Capstone Global Library Ltd
Printed and bound in China

17 16 15 14 13
10 9 8 7 6 5 4 3 2 1

Library of Congress Cataloging-in-Publication Data
Smith, Rupert, 1943-
  Poets of World War I / Rupert Smith.
    pages cm
  Includes bibliographical references and index.
  ISBN 978-1-4329-9645-1 (hb)—ISBN 978-1-4329-
9646-8 (pb) 1. World War, 1914-1918—Literature
and the war—Biography. 2. Poets, English—20th
century—Biography. 3. War poetry, English—His-
tory and criticism. 4. Soldiers' writings, English—
History and criticism. I. Title.
  PR605.W65S59 2014
  821'.91209358—dc23
2013015685
  [B]

Acknowledgments

We would like to thank the following for
permission to reproduce photographs: Alamy pp. 6
(Mirrorpix/© Trinity Mirror), 10 (© The Art Archive),
12 (© Maurice Savage), 18 (© The Art Archive), 20
(© The Art Archive), 31 (© Terry Harris), 34 (© The
Art Archive), 36 (© Everett Collection Historical), 47
(© Mary Evans Picture Library); Corbis pp. 16
(© Bettmann), 28 (© Michael Nicholson); Getty
Images pp. 8 (Hulton Archive/Phillips), 30 (Universal
History Archive), 32 (Popperfoto), 39 (Picture Post/
Bill Brandt), 40 (Hulton Archive); Harvard University
Archives p. 48 (HUD 3567.219.2, number 296);
© Imperial War Museums pp. 22 (Every effort has
been made to trace the copyright holder. The
author welcomes any information regarding the
copyright of this image.), 24, 26, 46 (The London
Rifle Brigade Collection); OUCS p. 14 (Image
provided by the Britten-Pears Foundation); Paul
Barlow p. 50; Photoshot pp. 44 (© UPPA), 55 (© E.O.
Hoppé); © The Royal Society p. 37; Shutterstock p. 4
(© Dziewul); SuperStock p. 53 (eps/Marka);
Westminster Abbey pic p. 5 (Copyright Dean and
Chapter of Westminster); The William Ready
Division of Archives and Research Collections,
McMaster University Library, p. 42. Vera Brittain
material is included by permission of Mark
Bostridge and T.J. Britain-Catlin, Literary Executors
for the Vera Brittain Estate 1970.

Cover photographs reproduced with permission of
Mary Evans Picture Library (Süddeutsche Zeitung
Photo) and Shutterstock (© Elena Elisseeva).

Every effort has been made to contact copyright
holders of material reproduced in this book. Any
omissions will be rectified in subsequent printings
if notice is given to the publisher.

All the Internet addresses (URLs) given in this book
were valid at the time of going to press. However,
due to the dynamic nature of the Internet, some
addresses may have changed, or sites may have
changed or ceased to exist since publication. While
the author and publisher regret any inconvenience
this may cause readers, no responsibility for any
such changes can be accepted by either the
author or the publisher.

CONTENTS

"MY SUBJECT IS WAR" 4

WILFRED OWEN 10

SIEGFRIED SASSOON 16

ISAAC ROSENBERG 22

RUPERT BROOKE 28

ROBERT GRAVES 34

VERA BRITTAIN 40

CHARLES SORLEY 44

ALAN SEEGER 48

OTHER VOICES 52

TIMELINE 56

FIND OUT MORE 59

GLOSSARY 60

NOTES ON SOURCES 62

INDEX 64

Any words appearing in the text in bold, **like this**, are explained in the glossary.

"MY SUBJECT IS WAR"

World War I was one of the bloodiest conflicts in modern history—and yet it produced some of the best poetry of the 20th century. The passion and power that readers find in the work of writers like Wilfred Owen and Alan Seeger make a very deep impact on them.

THE SHOCK OF WAR

What was it about the war that created such important poetry that we keep coming back to it 100 years later? There are three main answers to that question. First, World War I crashed into a world absolutely unprepared for slaughter on that scale. It was the first total "modern" war. It was fought with tanks and machine guns that were capable of wiping out tens of thousands of men in a day. At the time, much of the poetry was supportive of the war. But most of the war poetry we read today recorded the shock and disgust people felt for the sort of violence that, sadly, we now take for granted.

Second, the young men and women who wrote about the war were a very talented group of people. They were the product of a rich period of writing who suddenly found themselves inspired by an incredibly urgent subject matter. They wrote about it with great passion, from firsthand experience, but also with great artistry. They created work that spoke not only to readers at the time, but also to later generations.

PAIN INTO POETRY

Third, and perhaps most importantly, the war poets focused on issues that continue to matter to us today. They talked about the human cost of war and how politics played its part. They challenged governments, the public, and even the armed forces to justify the death and suffering of many millions.

When we read a poem like Owen's "Dulce et Decorum est" or Isaac Rosenberg's "Break of Day in the Trenches," we wonder how governments can possibly justify the wars that continue to plague our world. Some war poets—such as Owen, Rosenberg, and Seeger—died young. Some lived on, like Robert Graves, Siegfried Sassoon, and Ernest Hemingway. But they all summed up in their poetry the terror of fighting and witnessing destruction on a massive scale. Their voices will continue to be heard as long as nations find themselves at war.

A memorial stone in Westminster Abbey, London, United Kingdom, commemorates World War I poets. Owen's quote (see below) is in red.

LINK
See a large collection of material at the First World War Poetry Digital Archive:
www.oucs.ox.ac.uk/ww1lit

"My subject is War, and the pity of War. The Poetry is in the pity... All a poet can do today is warn. That is why the true Poets must be truthful."

Wilfred Owen, "**Preface**" (1918)

MAJOR THEMES

What was it like to live through World War I? Poetry is one of the most important records of how people felt about the life-changing events. As we read the poems, we see that there are some subjects that come up again and again. These were often things that were new, and shocking, to soldiers fighting at the front and to the people back home.

Sacrifice and glory

In the early months of the war, many men felt that joining the fight gave them a chance to do something wonderful for their country. Death was a small price to pay.

> " I am in a unit in the Great War, doing and suffering, admiring great endeavor and condemning great dishonor. I may be dead before this reaches you, but I will have done my part. Death is as interesting to me as life. "

Francis Ledwidge, Irish poet (1887–1917), written six months before his death at Ypres, Belgium[1]

Soldiers in a trench near the Somme River prepare for a gas attack with protective masks.

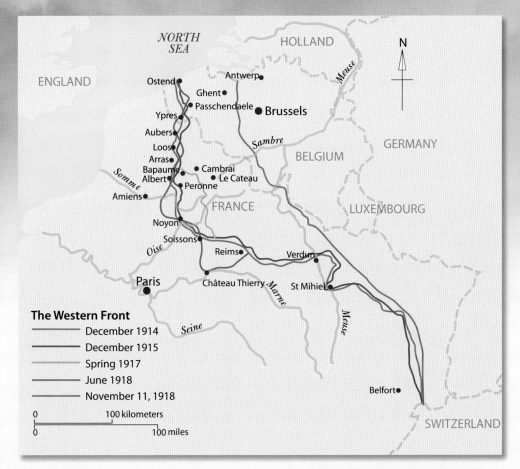

The Western Front
—— December 1914
—— December 1915
—— Spring 1917
—— June 1918
—— November 11, 1918

0   100 kilometers
0   100 miles

Trench warfare, shell shock, grief

World War I became a different type of fighting than anything seen before. The opposing armies dug into muddy trenches for many months and used barbed wire, **poison gas**, and machine guns. New inventions, including aircraft and tanks, gave them more efficient ways to kill each other.

Almost all of the poets in this book served on the **Western Front**—a line of trenches stretching from the North Sea coast of Belgium down through northeastern France to the Swiss border. Many of the main battles of World War I were fought along this line, in an attempt to halt German advances into France.

The **psychological** effects of trench warfare were unexpected and frightening. Many thousands of men were hospitalized with **shell shock**.

A few people, like the poet Charles Sorley, anticipated the horror of war. Most were unprepared for the scale of death and the grief that came in its wake. As a whole generation went to the slaughter, the mood of optimism turned to despair.

TIMES OF CHANGE

The years leading up to World War I saw incredible, rapid change. In industrial nations, such as the United States and Germany, people were enjoying increased prosperity. The **British Empire** was at its height, with money pouring in from all over the world. But political unrest was threatening the foundations of societies all over the world. This eventually led to the great shock of the **Russian Revolution** in 1917. The old way of life, where the upper class had all the money while the working class did all the labor, was breaking down. Better health and education encouraged ordinary people to demand better living standards for themselves and a greater share of the wealth. Women in the United States and Europe were campaigning for the right to vote. Many writers looked forward to war as a way to shake up society even more and make a fresh start.

Nothing, however, could prepare people for the reality of what became known as the Great War.

The calm before the storm: wealthy people in London enjoy a flower show in May 1914.

THEN and NOW

Life was very different in 1914. Life expectancy was a lot lower, and there were not many cars on the road. Women couldn't vote, and many of the freedoms that we take for granted today were a long way off. Here are some of the key facts about life in the United States then and now.

	Population	Life expectancy (years)	Women in work (%)	Average annual household income
1914	99,000,000[2]	54[4]	21.5[6]	$574[8]
Now	315,000,000[3]	77[5]	65[7]	$50,000[9]

A new type of war

There had been recent, bloody conflicts with enormous loss of life. In the United States, the Civil War (1861–1865) was still fresh in the memory of the older generation. The British had been fighting the Boer Wars against the Dutch in Africa as recently as 1902. But those wars were nothing compared with World War I. The scale of death was unimaginable—which was partly due to new technology. Machines were providing jobs for millions, better transportation, and an easier way of life. But they were also creating new, more efficient ways of killing. Tanks, machine guns, poison gas, and aerial bombs replaced rifles and swords as the tools of modern war.

It was also hard to figure out what the fighting was for. A few yards of mud in northeast France? What did that matter to anyone? Things were very different in World War II, when people understood the threat of Adolf Hitler. But to a soldier in 1916, facing certain death in the trenches, progress seemed slow and the results uncertain. Religion was breaking down, church attendance was plummeting, and the war seemed to confirm that we were living in a godless world. After the horrors of the Western Front, nothing would ever be the same again.

> **LINK**
> Find out more about life in the United States in the period before and during the war at kclibrary.lonestar.edu/decade10.html

WILFRED OWEN

Born: Oswestry, Shropshire, England, 1893
Died: Ors, France, 1918

Wilfred Owen wrote some of the most famous poems of World War I, including "Anthem for Doomed Youth," "Dulce et Decorum est," and "Strange Meeting."

DID YOU KNOW?
Owen was killed just one week before the end of the war.

Wilfred Owen was 25 when he died in France.[10] He spent a total of four months in active service, of which not more than five weeks were at the front line. But despite his youth and relative lack of experience, Owen has become among the best known of all the war poets—and his reputation keeps on growing. More than any of his **contemporaries**, he represents the tragedy, the anger, and the terrible sense of waste that draws us back to the war poets 100 years later.

BEFORE THE WAR

Wilfred was the oldest of four children. His father was a railroad employee who struggled to provide for the family. When Wilfred was 14, the family moved to Shrewsbury, England. The teenage Wilfred developed an interest in poetry, especially the work of the English poets John Keats and Percy Bysshe Shelley.

Wilfred's parents couldn't afford to send him to college, and so he took an unpaid job as an assistant to a local church leader. Under the influence of his very religious mother, he was thinking of becoming a church minister.

WRITING ON THE FRONT LINE

Owen eventually left the church to work as an English teacher in France. The outbreak of war found him in Bordeaux, France, cultivating friendships with French poets and writing his own work in his spare time. In September 1915, a full year after the start of the war, Owen could stand aside no longer. He returned to England and **enlisted**. "I don't imagine that the German War will be affected by my joining in," he wrote to his cousin Leslie Gunston, "but I know my own future Peace will be." [11]

For the next 14 months, he trained as an officer. It wasn't until the end of 1916 that he was finally posted to France on active service. He was **commissioned** as a second lieutenant within his regiment, a junior officer leading his men in the very worst of the fighting.[12] For two short, intense periods—winter 1916 to spring 1917, and summer to fall 1918—Owen witnessed the horrors of trench warfare (see page 14). He was still writing all the time, sending poems home in letters to his friends and family in England.

Getting recognized

Owen was regarded by his admirers as a writer of great promise. But it was only after the end of the war that his friend and champion Siegfried Sassoon edited and published the first collected edition of Owen's work. His poetry has never been out of print since then.

"One of Christ's essential commands was: Passivity at any price! Suffer dishonor and disgrace; but never resort to arms... Be killed; but do not kill... And am I not myself a **conscientious objector** with a very seared conscience?"

Letter from Wilfred Owen to his mother, Susan Owen (May 1917) [13]

LINK
The Wilfred Owen Association has information and news about Wilfred Owen's life at www.wilfredowen.org.uk

OWEN'S WAR

Owen's first experience of action was on the Somme River in France, in January 1917. The **Allies** were holding a stretch of **no-man's-land** in Beaumont-Hamel. It was a dangerous place for an inexperienced young officer to be. "I have suffered seventh hell," Owen wrote to his mother. "I have not been at the Front. I have been in front of it."[14]

Away from the protection of the trenches, he led his men across a land of mud—"not sloppy mud, but an octopus of sucking clay, 3, 4, and 5 feet deep, relieved only by craters full of water. Men have been known to drown in them." They took refuge in a dug-out (a hole in the ground used as a temporary shelter) while the Germans shelled them. He wrote: "My dug-out held 25 men tightly packed. Water filled it to a depth of 1 or 2 feet, leaving say 4 feet of air." Owen survived, but he witnessed terrible **carnage**.

Illness and injury

Over the coming months, Owen suffered from a concussion and illness as a result of the cold, wet conditions from when he was sent repeatedly to the line. Finally, on April 12, 1917, he was hit by a shell. He spent several days taking shelter in a hole with the remains of a dead officer.

Owen was diagnosed with **shell shock**. He was evacuated to the Craiglockhart War Hospital near Edinburgh, Scotland, to recover. It was during this time that he met Siegfried Sassoon (see page 15).

 Owen's grave in the communal cemetery in Ors, northern France, is close to the spot where he was killed.

LINK

To find out more about what life was like in the trenches, visit www.firstworldwar.com/features/trenchlife.htm

"The sensations of going **over the top** are about as exhilarating as those dreams of falling over a precipice, when you see the rocks at the bottom surging up to you. I woke up without being squashed. Some didn't."

Letter from Wilfred Owen to his brother Colin (May 14, 1917)

Owen was discharged from the hospital in October 1917, and he considered looking for a posting at home in England for the rest of the war. However, Sassoon's decision to return to the front convinced Owen to rejoin his regiment in France. Sassoon was wounded, and Owen was determined to carry on his work, writing: "Now must I throw my little candle on his torch, and go out again."[15] He left England on August 31, 1918, never to return.

Brave ending

The fortunes of war were changing. Germany's final offensive had failed, and the Allied forces were pushing them toward surrender. Owen was in the thick of it and was awarded the **Military Cross** for his bravery in battle. He continued writing, sending his final batch of poems to Sassoon in September. It included "**Spring Offensive**," one of his finest poems.

Owen was killed during an assault on the Sambre–Oise canal near Ors, France, on November 4, 1918. A telegram bearing the news of his death reached his family a week later, on **Armistice** Day.

DISCUSSION TOPIC

Why did Owen fight?

It is obvious from his poetry that Owen was disgusted by the war. Yet he not only enlisted in the first place, but returned to the battlefield after recovering from shell shock. Why do you think he went back to France?

OWEN'S POETRY

One of the reasons why Owen remains among the most popular of all war poets is his talent for putting complex, painful ideas into simple but powerful language. His religious background equipped him with imagery that he used to great effect, and war gave him subject matter.

The poems from Owen's early trench experience, such as "Greater Love," are highly **romantic** and emotional. The turning point in his style came when he met Siegfried Sassoon in August 1917. Sassoon encouraged Owen to write in a harsher, more direct style and to abandon the lush imagery of earlier work. The effect was immediate.

An original manuscript written by Owen in 1917 shows Sassoon's notes and suggestions. The word *Dead* in the title was later changed to *Doomed*.

LINK

Find out more about how Owen wrote his poetry at the British Library web site: www.bl.uk/learning/langlit/changlang/writtenword/owenpoem/owenhome.html

"Gas! GAS! Quick, boys!—An ecstasy of fumbling,

Fitting the clumsy helmets just in time;

But someone still was yelling out and stumbling,

And flound'ring like a man in fire or lime...

Dim, through the misty panes and thick green light,

As under a green sea, I saw him drowning."

"Dulce et Decorum est" (1917)

Rage and grief

The poems that Owen wrote in the last 15 months of his life were brutal, sometimes funny, and often heartbreaking. He used the real speech of soldiers—for example, "I'll do 'em in," says the soldier in "The Dead-Beat," the first poem he wrote "in Sassoon's style."[16] His first masterpiece, "Anthem for Doomed Youth," was written in Edinburgh in September 1917. In 14 lines, it expresses the rage and grief that Owen felt after witnessing the slaughter of his comrades.

Owen came to hate the false **patriotism** that was sending young men to certain death. He expresses this idea in his angriest poem, "Dulce et Decorum est." It portrays the horrific events of a gas attack before challenging the reader to repeat "the old lie" in the title—"*Dulce et decorum est pro patria mori*" (or "How sweet and right it is to die for one's country"). This and Owen's final poems, including "The **Show**," "S. I. W.," "Mental Cases," "Strange Meeting," and "Spring Offensive," are among the most famous works of the war.

OWEN AND SASSOON

When Owen met Siegfried Sassoon in 1917, this was one of the key moments in the history of war poetry. Owen knew of and admired Sassoon's work, writing to his mother, "I am not worthy to light his pipe."[17] But later, Sassoon admitted that perhaps Owen was the greater poet.[18] Their friendship has inspired many writers and shows how influential writers can be for each other.

SIEGFRIED SASSOON

Born: Matfield, Kent, England, 1886
Died: Heytesbury Hall, Wiltshire, England, 1967

Siegfried Sassoon was a fierce critic of the war who expressed his anger, sorrow, and frustration in some of the most powerful poetry of the period.

DID YOU KNOW?
Sassoon survived the trenches and wrote several best-selling books after the war. He lived to the age of 80.

Siegfried Sassoon came from a rich, upper-class family in England.[19] His early life was idyllic—he didn't start school until he was 14, and he seemed more interested in playing sports, hunting, and writing poetry than getting into college. The only clouds on the horizon were the breakup of his parents' marriage and the death of his father. However, he inherited a lot of money from his aunt and lived the life of a wealthy country gentleman.

The outbreak of war in 1914 jolted Sassoon out of his comfortable existence. He **enlisted** right away. The conflict touched his family deeply when his brother Hamo was killed at **Gallipoli** in 1915. Sassoon quickly established a reputation for bravery (his men nicknamed him "Mad Jack"). He recorded his impressions of war in his poems.

"FINISHED WITH THE WAR"

Sassoon's attitude to the war changed quickly. At first he was as enthusiastic as everyone else, but by 1916 he had become critical of the fact that soldiers were being sent to certain death. During a stay in England in 1917, Sassoon wrote a letter to his commanding officer under the heading: "Finished with the War: A Soldier's Declaration." He wrote: "I am making this statement as an act of wilful defiance of military authority, because I believe that the war is being deliberately prolonged by those who have the power to end it."[20] The letter was printed in newspapers and read during a meeting of the UK government. Sassoon narrowly avoided being **court-martialed**. He was sent instead to Craiglockhart War Hospital in Edinburgh, Scotland, officially suffering from **shell shock**.

The scandal made Sassoon famous. His war poems, mainly published in 1917 and 1918, sold widely. In 1919, Sassoon left the army. Later that year, *War Poems* was published, sealing his reputation as the most critical and **satirical** of all the poets of the period.

After the war, Sassoon suffered from depression. It was not until 1928, with the autobiographical *Memoirs of a Fox-Hunting Man*, that he again found his way as a writer. Despite the success of his books, he was unfulfilled and had a string of failed relationships. In 1951, he received the award of Commander of the Order of the **British Empire** (the third-highest honor for service during World War I). Sassoon died in 1967, at the age of 80.

LINK

Read more at the Siegfried Sassoon Fellowship: **www.sassoonfellowship.org**

> "I believe that this war, on which I entered as a war of defense and liberation, has now become a war of aggression and conquest."
>
> "Finished with the War: A Soldier's Declaration" (1917)

Sassoon's letters, notes, and poems from the front record his changing attitude toward the war.

HERO OR TRAITOR?

Sassoon was 27 when war was declared, and with his upper-class background, it was obvious that he would be **commissioned** as an officer.[21] In 1914, he enlisted as a trooper, but by 1915, he was a second lieutenant. He was sent almost right away to France, where he immediately became a hero to his men for rescuing a wounded soldier under heavy fire. For this action, Sassoon was awarded the **Military Cross**. Later that year, he took a German trench single-handedly and was recommended for the highest military award for bravery, the Victoria Cross.

> "As I stepped over one of the Germans an impulse made me lift him up from the miserable ditch... He didn't look to be more than 18. Hoisting him a little higher, I thought what a gentle face he had, and remembered that this was the first time I'd ever touched one of our enemies with my hands."

Description of the Battle of the Somme, *Memoirs of an Infantry Officer* (1930)[22]

Sassoon's attitude toward the war changed in 1916, when he witnessed the first **Battle of the Somme** in July and the bloody Battle of Arras in April of the following year. These experiences, combined with the deaths of people close to him, made Sassoon question the war. While recovering from his injuries in 1917, Sassoon decided that his duty as a writer was to tell people about the pointless **carnage** he had witnessed.

Changing his mind

Many people branded Sassoon a traitor for opposing the war, but nobody could question his bravery. Sassoon himself rejected the title of hero—he threw the ribbon from his Military Cross medal into a river in England, intending never to return to battle.[23] But he changed his mind while he was in the hospital, and in November 1917, he was declared fit for "general service" and returned to duty. He stayed at the front line in France until July, when he was shot in the head by a British soldier who had mistaken him for a German.[24] The wound was not serious, but it was bad enough to end his active service.

DISCUSSION TOPIC

Was Sassoon a traitor?
Sassoon published outspoken criticism of the war and the people who were running it in the government and the army, at the height of conflict. Was he right or wrong to do so? Would it have been different if someone had made the same criticisms in World War II?

LINK
Find out more about Sassoon's wartime experiences at the War Poets Association web site: **www.warpoets.org/conflicts/greatwar/sassoon**

THE RELUCTANT WAR POET

The label "war poet" annoyed Siegfried Sassoon, who wrote poems both before and after World War I. However, he is best known for his 100 or so poems that deal with the war. Wilfred Owen regarded him as a hero and an inspiration, calling him "the Greatest friend I have."[25] Sassoon's angry, satirical verse defines what many now think of as war poetry.

Sassoon started writing poetry in his teenage years and attracted the attention of influential critics and editors—but he realized that he had not yet found his true subject matter. That came with the war and the shocking death of his brother Hamo and close friend David Thomas, both of whom he commemorated in poems ("To My Brother," "A Subaltern," and "The Last Meeting").

Sassoon met the poet Robert Graves while on duty in France in 1916. Graves encouraged Sassoon to write in a more direct, less "poetic" style, just as Sassoon did with Owen a year later. Sassoon began reporting what he saw in a vivid, factual way—the best way, he thought, to bring his message to readers back home. He wrote "Died of Wounds" in a hospital at Amiens, France, in 1916. It is a brief, brutal description of a young soldier's final hours.[26] "They" (1916) was written in a fit of anger: "George lost both his legs; and Bill's stone blind; / Poor Jim's shot through the lungs and like to die." Even Sassoon's editor, Edward Marsh, thought it "too horrible."[27]

British soldiers go over the top in the Battle of the Somme, as described in Sassoon's poem "Attack."

PACIFISM IN WORLD WAR I

Not everyone believed that war was justified, and some people refused to fight. This meant they were breaking the law—and many of them ended up in prison as a result. Many thought they were cowards, but there was a growing number of prominent figures in the United States and Europe who believed in **pacifism**—peace above all else. Today, some people choose to wear white poppies instead of the traditional red, as a way of remembering the dead while expressing their opposition to war.

"COUNTER-ATTACK"

Sassoon published many of his most important pieces in two books, *The Old Huntsman* (1917) and *Counter-Attack* (1918). Even before the scandal of "Finished with the War" (see page 17), these poems were a shock to readers. "Attack" (1917) remains the most powerful expression of going **over the top**. "Counter-Attack" (1917) perfectly summed up Sassoon's anger at the waste of life. After a horrific, dramatic account of trench warfare ("The place was rotten with dead"), he watches another soldier bleed to death before recording, in the last line, "The counter-attack had failed."

One of Sassoon's last war poems, written after the **armistice**, is "Everyone Sang"—proof that he could write about more than just misery. It ends very sadly: "the song was wordless." Yet his joy at the end of the war ("I was filled with such delight / As prisoned birds must find in freedom") is a rare moment of light in the very dark landscape of his work.

> "Lines of grey, muttering faces, masked with fear,
> They leave their trenches, going over the top,
> While time ticks blank and busy on their wrists,
> And hope, with furtive eyes and grappling fists,
> Flounders in mud. O Jesus, make it stop!"

"Attack" (1917)

LINK

Listen to recordings of Sassoon reading his war poetry at the Poetry Archive:
www.poetryarchive.org/poetryarchive/singlePoet.do?poetId=1561

ISAAC ROSENBERG

Born: Bristol, England, 1890
Died: Fampoux, France, 1918

Isaac Rosenberg overcame health problems and a lack of education to become one of the most important poets of the war before his death on the **Western Front**.

DID YOU KNOW?
Rosenberg **enlisted** in the **Bantam** Battalion of his regiment because it was for men under 5 feet, 3 inches (1.6 meters) tall.

Isaac Rosenberg is unique among the war poets. The son of **Jewish immigrants**, he grew up in poverty in London. He was a small, sickly young man who believed in **pacifism** and only enlisted because his soldier's pay would keep his family from starving.[28] He was also a talented artist. His poems are often described as difficult and obscure—and yet Rosenberg is now considered among the best of the war poets.

EARLY LIFE

Isaac's street peddler father fled Russia to raise his growing family in England. In 1897, the family moved to Cable Street in London, where both parents and five children slept in one room.

Isaac had a gift for painting and drawing, but he had to leave school at 14 to start earning money. He became an apprentice engraver and went to evening art classes. In 1911, he gained a place at the famous Slade School of Fine Art in London.

POET OR PAINTER?

Throughout his time at Slade, Rosenberg was writing as well as painting, but he was never confident about his literary talent. "I really would like to take up painting seriously," he wrote in 1910, "I think I might do something at that; but poetry—I despair of ever writing excellent poetry."[29] By the time Rosenberg left art school in 1913, he had attracted the attention of Edward Marsh, the powerful editor of the book *Georgian Poetry*, which included work by Siegfried Sassoon and Rupert Brooke.

In 1914, Rosenberg traveled to South Africa to recover from the chronic bronchitis that affected him all his life. The warm weather helped, but he was unlucky—war was declared, and he returned to England. He enlisted and was posted right to the Somme in 1916.

Rosenberg was 27 years old when he died. His poetry was just starting to gain international recognition. Rosenberg himself believed at the end of his life that he was "more deep and true as a poet than painter."[30] His most enduring work was not published until years later. His paintings now hang in some of the most important galleries in the world.

> "I think that poetry should be definite thought and clear expression, however subtle; I don't think there should be any vagueness at all; but a sense of something hidden and felt to be there."
>
> Letter from Isaac Rosenberg to Edward Marsh (1917)[31]

LINK

Find out more about Rosenberg and his poetry at
www.poetryfoundation.org/bio/isaac-rosenberg

AN UNKNOWN GENIUS

The Road is a 1911 painting by Rosenberg from the time he started training at the Slade School of Fine Art.

Some of Rosenberg's poems and **fragments** were published before his death, but it wasn't until 1937, with the publication of his *Collected Works*, that he became widely read. Siegfried Sassoon was a great admirer of Rosenberg's poetry. He wrote a foreword to the book, hoping "to gain for him the full recognition of his genius which has hitherto been delayed."[32]

Rosenberg realized that his work would not appeal to everyone. He wrote in a letter in 1915: "Most people find my poems difficult. My technique in poetry is very clumsy, I know."[33] Rosenberg was deeply immersed in Jewish culture and history, and at first he focused on Biblical themes.

The war gave Rosenberg a much more urgent subject matter. It also forced him to use a more direct style: writing at the front, he just didn't have time to polish his poems. He wrote: "You can only, when the ideas come hot, seize them with the skin in tatters raw, crude, in some parts beautiful, in others monstrous."[34]

WRITING IN THE TRENCHES

Between 1915 and his death in 1918, Rosenberg wrote the poems that made him famous after he died. Sassoon, among others, considered "Break of Day in the Trenches" to be one of the best poems of the war. It is a strangely calm, intimate piece of writing that sums up Rosenberg's approach. He focuses on a rat that runs across his hand: "You will do the same to a German / Soon, no doubt." As he watches the rat disappear across **no-man's-land**, he wonders, "What do you see in our eyes / At the shrieking iron and flame." Finally, Rosenberg picks a poppy from the top of the trench and sticks it behind his ear— a simple act of defiance to the horror that would soon claim his life.

His poems "Louse Hunting" and "Dead Man's Dump" are equal in power to anything by Owen or Sassoon. They suggest that Rosenberg was capable of achieving great things. Sassoon wrote, "I see the poems he might have written after the war, and the life he might have lived when life began again."[35] Sadly, unlike Sassoon, Rosenberg never had the chance to prove his potential.

> "The air is loud with death,
> The dark air spurts with fire
> The explosions ceaseless are.
> Timelessly now, some minutes past,
> These dead strode time with vigorous life,
> Till the shrapnel called 'an end!'"
>
> "Dead Man's Dump" (1917)

DISCUSSION TOPIC

Rosenberg the outsider

Unlike most British war poets, who were well-off, native Englishmen, Rosenberg came from working-class Jewish immigrants and was a soldier, not an officer. How did his "outsider" status influence his poetry? Can we tell from his work that his background was different?

"I have joined this Bantam Battalion (as I was too short for any other) which seems to be the most rascally affair in the world. I have to eat out of a basin with some horribly smelling scavenger... Besides my being a Jew makes it bad amongst these wretches. I am looking forward to having a bad time altogether."

Letter from Isaac Rosenberg to his friend Sydney Schiff (October 1915)[36]

Casualties in the Battle of the Somme[37]	
Nationality	Numbers
British	Approximately 420,000
French	Approximately 195,000
German	Approximately 650,000

Battle fatigue: English soldiers rest during the Battle of the Somme, their rifles stacked nearby. Exhaustion and **shell shock** put many of them in the hospital.

THE MOST DANGEROUS PLACE ON EARTH

Rosenberg arrived in France at the worst possible time—right in the middle of the **Battle of the Somme**.[38] He missed the disastrous massacre of the first few days, but when he was sent to the trenches at the end of August 1916, the Somme was still the most dangerous place on earth. His chances of survival were very low. Even the most pro-war newspapers were beginning to admit that the number of **casualties** in France was far greater than had ever been predicted.

Rosenberg served in the trenches of the Somme for five months. He witnessed the full impact of war at close quarters. He wrote about what he saw in poems and letters, but he said very little about the conditions at the front. He sometimes mentioned the cold and the wet, but he was only really interested in his work. "Winter is not the least of the horrors of war," he wrote to the poet Laurence Binyon toward the end of 1916, as he was freezing in the trenches. "I am determined that this war, with all its powers for devastation, shall not master my poeting; this is, if I am lucky enough to come through it all right."[39]

Spring Offensive

Rosenberg's health broke down at the beginning of 1917. For much of that year, he was in and out of the hospital, suffering from bronchitis and the flu. During that time, he worked furiously on poems and plays, encouraged by the recognition that his writing was getting from influential critics. However, at the end of the year, he was declared fit enough to return to the front. December saw him once again in the trenches, and he remained there, with occasional rests behind the lines, until his death.

On April 1, 1918, during the German **Spring Offensive**, Rosenberg was on night patrol near the town of Fampoux, France, on the Western Front. He was killed at dawn, possibly by a **sniper**'s bullet, possibly in close combat. He was buried in a mass grave. In 1926, his body was discovered and identified along with 10 others from his regiment. His remains now rest in the Bailleul Road East Cemetery, Saint-Laurent-Blangy, near Arras, in northern France.

> **LINK**
> The Commonwealth War Graves Commission is a searchable database of war cemeteries, including Rosenberg's burial place: **www.cwgc.org**

Rupert Brooke

Born: Rugby, Warwickshire, England, 1887
Died: Skyros, Greece, 1915

Rupert Brooke rocketed to fame in 1915 when his poem "The Soldier" was read aloud in St. Paul's Cathedral in London, just a few months before his death. His work inspired thousands of young men to **enlist**.

DID YOU KNOW?
Brooke died from blood poisoning resulting from an infected mosquito bite.

Rupert Brooke was famous for his good looks as well as his poetry before the war broke out. He became one of the most celebrated figures of his generation after his death at the age of 27.

His father, William Brooke, was in charge of boarding students at an important private school in England. Rupert was the second of three sons. He had a happy, secure childhood and was a star athlete and excellent student. He even won prizes for his poetry. It was obvious to everyone that Rupert would go far. "Almost everyone came under the sway of his personality,"[40] wrote his schoolfriend Hugh Russell-Smith.

In 1906, Brooke went to the University of Cambridge to study Classics (the works of ancient cultures such as ancient Rome and Greece). Here, too, he quickly attracted attention. He acted in plays and wrote poetry.

Brooke campaigned on behalf of political groups that believed in equal distribution of wealth. He was elected to the Cambridge Apostles, an influential "secret society." This brought him into contact with some of the major artists and thinkers of his generation.

Brooke spent his summer vacations touring Europe and visiting friends in London. He soon became involved with the Bloomsbury Group, a circle of artists and writers who were the major creative force in England at the time. His first book, *Poems*, was published in 1911, when he was 24. He was well on the way to becoming famous.

"DREAMS OF GLORY"

Later, Brooke suffered from illness and a series of failed relationships, which led to a breakdown in 1913. He spent much of that year traveling in North America, returning to England via Fiji and Tahiti. He got home just before the outbreak of war and enlisted right away, spurred on by **patriotism**. He received a **commission** from Winston Churchill, then a leader in the British navy.

As early as October 1914, Brooke was sailing to Europe. He was sent to Antwerp, in Belgium, where he witnessed some shelling but little in the way of direct action. "When they told us...that we were all going to be killed in Antwerp," he wrote in a letter,[41] "I thought 'what Hell it is that I shan't have any children'... And we were barely even under fire, in the end!"

> "A young Apollo, golden-haired,
> Stands dreaming on the verge of strife,
> Magnificently unprepared
> For the long littleness of life."
>
> *On Rupert Brooke*, Frances Cornford (1910)

LINK

Find out more about Rupert Brooke at the Poetry Foundation web site: www.poetryfoundation.org/bio/rupert-brooke

Brooke must have been excited to be selected as part of the mission to the **Dardanelles** in 1915. The objective was simple: to capture the city of Constantinople (modern Istanbul) from Turkey. This would create a safe route for **Allied** ships to Russia. "It's too wonderful for belief," he wrote on hearing the news.[42] "I'm filled with confident and glorious hopes."

Dead before battle

The Dardanelles campaign was a disaster. It culminated in the Battle of **Gallipoli** (April 1915 to January 1916) with massive **casualties** on both sides. It was one of the turning points in attitudes toward the war.

Brooke never made it to the battle. On February 28, 1915, he sailed from Bristol into the Mediterranean and along the north African coast. He seemed to be in a dream world. "We've had rather a nice voyage," he wrote in March, "very smooth and delicious."[43]

Rupert Brooke's movie star good looks made him popular during his lifetime and even more famous after his death in 1915.

On April 17, the ship landed on the Greek island of Skyros. Four days later, Brooke became sick with a temperature of 103 degrees. He was transferred to a French hospital ship moored in the Aegean Sea, but it was too late: he died of blood poisoning on April 23.

"ENGLAND'S NOBLEST SON"

Brooke's story does not end there. Three days after his death, Winston Churchill wrote a letter to *The Times* newspaper praising Brooke's poetry and describing him as "all that one could wish England's noblest sons to be."[44] It is this image that ensured the poet's immortality.

> "During the last few months of his life...the poet-soldier told with all the simple force of genius the sorrow of youth about to die... He expected to die: he was willing to die for the dear England whose beauty and majesty he knew."
>
> Brooke's obituary by Winston Churchill, *The Times*, April 26, 1915[45]

MEMORIAL

Rupert Brooke was buried in a simple grave with stones and a wooden cross. Shortly after the war, his mother commissioned a more permanent grave to be built on the same site, adding an inscription from "The Soldier" to it. In 1931, an additional memorial was built in Skyros Town, featuring a statue of an "ideal poet."[46]

ENGLAND DECLARES WAR ON GERMANY—
1. CHIPPING NORTON TERRITORIALS GOING ON SERVICE. AUG 5. 19

"THE SOLDIER"

Rupert Brooke's poem "The Soldier" was
published in *The Times*, where it reached
a massive audience.[47] Its **romantic**, **idealistic**

Early volunteers were
sent off on a wave of
patriotic fervor, which
was depicted in Brooke's
poetry. Few returned.

vision of a soldier-hero sacrificing himself for his country perfectly
summed up England's mood at the time, before the true cost of the
conflict was revealed. Brooke's reputation, both good and bad, rests
mostly on that poem. The opening lines are far removed from the
realistic poetry of Sassoon and Owen. Many have criticized Brooke for
avoiding the horror of war, and for valuing patriotism and glory more
than human suffering.

It is certainly true that Brooke's poetry has little in common with the
mud, blood, and pain described by his **contemporaries**. But that is
not to say that he was deliberately ignoring them. Brooke died in April
1915, before the disaster of Gallipoli and the massive casualties on
the **Western Front**. He died before the hard facts of trench warfare
were known. None of the other poets had written anything serious
or angry by this time, either. It is possible that Brooke, had he lived,

would have changed his attitude to the war. Given his liberal politics and connections with those who embraced **pacifism**, it is likely that he would have become as much a critic of the war as Sassoon and Owen.

> "If I should die, think only this of me:
> That there's some corner of a foreign field
> That is for ever England. There shall be
> In that rich earth a richer dust concealed;
> A dust whom England bore, shaped, made aware"
>
> "The Soldier" (1914)

Other poetry

Brooke wrote another famous poem, "The Old Vicarage, Grantchester," in May 1912 in Berlin, Germany. He was terribly homesick and depressed, and the intensity of his longing for home bursts out of every line, most famously the final couplet: "Stands the Church clock at ten to three? / And is there honey still for tea?" But alongside that sweet nostalgia, some sadness comes out in other poems—for example, "A Channel Passage" with its description of seasickness, and "The Fish," which is a **satire** on religion.

But it is "The Soldier" and the four other 1914 sonnets that make Brooke an important war poet. More than any other writer, he expressed the national feeling in England in the early months of World War I. His words inspired and comforted many soldiers and their families.

LINK
You can read all of Rupert Brooke's poems online at the Rupert Brooke Society web site: www.rupertbrooke.com

DISCUSSION TOPIC

Did Brooke glorify war?
Brooke's poetry makes going to war and dying for your country sound heroic and glorious. It is a different interpretation of war than that found in Owen and Sassoon's later poetry, but does that make Brooke a worse poet? Do you think Brooke's attitude toward war would have changed, like Sassoon's, if he had seen action?

ROBERT GRAVES

Born: Wimbledon, London, England, 1895
Died: Majorca, Spain, 1985

Robert Graves was the first of the major World War I poets to publish his work. He survived the war and went on to have a hugely successful career as a poet and novelist.

DID YOU KNOW?
Graves's novel *I, Claudius* was the basis for a popular TV series from the 1970s.

Of all the war poets, it is Robert Graves who went on to have the most successful career. He was one of the lucky ones: despite one very near miss, he survived the trenches. By the late 1920s, Graves was an internationally famous writer.

Robert Graves was born into a middle-class family. His mother, Amalie von Ranke, was German.[48] The worsening political situation in Europe meant that anti-German feeling was running high. High school for Robert was a nightmare. He was bullied because of his mother's nationality and his own strong, artistic temperament. He became isolated and deeply unhappy. Then war was declared when Graves was 19, so he **enlisted** immediately.[49]

Poetic pioneer

Graves's first volume of poems, *Over the Brazier*, was published in 1916. It gained attention for its realistic tone, which was very different from the lush, sentimental style that was in fashion. In France, Graves became friends with Siegfried Sassoon, and he influenced Sassoon's writing style (see page 20).

Graves was badly wounded at the **Battle of the Somme** and spent most of the rest of the war in England and Ireland. He married Nancy Nicholson just before the **Armistice** in 1918. He attended the University of Oxford and continued writing. He and Nancy had four children.

His first marriage ended, and Graves settled on the Spanish island of Majorca. He had four more children with his second wife, Beryl Pritchard. By now he was a literary celebrity: his autobiography, *Good-Bye to All That* (1929), recounted his war experiences and his friendships with Sassoon and Owen.

Successful author

Graves never stopped writing poetry, and there is no doubt that it was his greatest love. But he is best known for his prose. In 1934, he published *I, Claudius*, a fictionalized account of the life of the Roman emperor. It was a global best-seller. His nonfiction writings on history and mythology, particularly *The Greek Myths* (1955), were also popular.

In later life, Graves suffered from memory loss. He was unable to write much after the age of 80. He survived for a further 10 years and was buried near his home on Majorca.

> "It's hard to know if you're alive or dead
> When steel and fire go roaring through your head."
>
> "It's a Queer Time" (1915)

LINK
For more on the life and work of Robert Graves, see **www.robertgraves.org**

REPORTED DEAD

Graves enlisted as a soldier in 1914 full of **patriotic** enthusiasm. He was excited to be going to war and unaware of what he would find when he got there.

Military hospitals had to treat a wide range of injuries as well as psychological conditions. Many were basic, makeshift setups like this one set up in a church in France, around 1917.

It did not take him long to find out. Graves recalled his trench experience in his postwar autobiography *Good-Bye to All That*, one of the most important records of what life was like for soldiers serving at the front. "The trench was cut through red clay," he wrote of his first day. "I had a torch [flashlight] with me which I kept flashed on the ground. Hundreds of field mice and frogs were in the trench. They had fallen in and had no way out. The light dazzled them and we could not help treading on them. So I put the torch back in my pocket."[50]

On July 20, 1916, just before his 21st birthday, Graves was hit by a shell **fragment**. It entered his shoulder and chest, hitting his right lung and very nearly killing him. His death was reportedly announced in *The Times* newspaper, much to the distress of his family, who only found out that he was still alive when he came back to England.

Shell shock and after

An injured lung was not Graves's only problem: he was suffering from **shell shock**. He made a full recovery from his physical injuries, but the **psychological** aftereffects stayed with him for at least 10 years.

Once he had left the hospital, Graves was eager to get back to the front. He secured a posting to France, only to be told by his company doctor that he was not fit for action. He was sent home and threatened with a **court martial** if he disobeyed.[51]

Graves spent the rest of the war in noncombat service, mostly training troops for the front. "I thought of going back to France," he wrote, "but realized the absurdity of the notion. Since 1916, the fear of gas obsessed me: any unusual smell, even a sudden strong smell of flowers in a garden, was enough to send me trembling. And I couldn't face the sound of heavy shelling now; the noise of a car back-firing would send me flat on my face, or running for cover."[52]

W. H. R. Rivers (1864–1922) was a pioneering doctor. He was one of the first to use **psychoanalysis** to address the problems of men who had served in the trenches. Graves met Rivers when he escorted Siegfried Sassoon for treatment for shell shock at Craiglockhart War Hospital (see page 17). Graves himself was not treated by Rivers, but he was interested in the doctor's ideas on the mental process of writing poetry.[53]

"Another war soon gets begun,
A dirtier, a more glorious one
Then, boys, you'll have to play, all in;
It's the cruellest team will win.
So hold your nose against the stink
And never stop too long to think.
Wars don't change except in name;
The next one must go just the same."

"The Next War" (1917)

REPORTING FROM THE FRONT

Graves was the first British war poet to write about his experiences in direct, sometimes brutal language without any flowery, "poetic" touches. His book *Over the Brazier* contains work he mostly wrote at the front. It is a stark contrast to the work of Rupert Brooke. It is written in everyday language that other soldiers would understand, and it does not avoid unpleasant realities. Siegfried Sassoon, who was serving in the same battalion, was very influenced by Graves's work.

Graves knew that what he was doing was different. In 1940, he wrote an article about the poetry of World War I that described the work of Rupert Brooke and other early war poets as "gallant and **idealistic** but with hardly a real poet among them."[54] The change, he said, came in 1917, with the realization that too many people were dying for no good reason. This was exactly when Sassoon and Owen started writing their best work.

Graves was being modest: he had already gotten there two years earlier. In July 1915, he wrote one of his best-known poems, "A Dead Boche." It describes his discovery of a dead body in a wood. (*Boche* is a slang word for "German.") He wrote: "Propped up against a shattered trunk, / In a great mess of things unclean, / Sat a dead Boche... Dribbling black blood from nose and beard."

MOVING ON FROM WAR

Most of Graves's war poetry was published in three volumes—
Over the Brazier and *Goliath and David* (1916), and *Fairies and
Fusiliers* (1917). He returned to the subject often in later life, as he
struggled to come to terms with what had happened to him. But it is
his war poems that built his reputation.

Graves's work is not always easy to read. It is nowhere near as
emotional or angry as that of Owen and Sassoon, which explains why it
is not as famous. Unlike Sassoon, Graves managed to move on from the
war and find new, bigger subjects. He was thinking, perhaps, of some
of his fellow poets when he wrote the bittersweet poem "When I'm
Killed," writing: "So when I'm killed, don't wait for me... You'll find me
buried, living-dead / In these verses that you've read."

Robert Graves
was a very
successful author
by the time this
photo was taken,
in 1941.

LINK

Read more of Graves's wartime
experiences in extracts from his
1929 autobiography *Good-Bye to
All That* at **projects.oucs.ox.ac.uk/
jtap/rose/goodbye.html**

DISCUSSION TOPIC

Stark language
Why did Robert Graves decide
to write about the war in
such simple, straightforward
language? And why was this such
a big influence on other poets?

VERA BRITTAIN

Born: Buxton, Derbyshire, England, 1893

Died: Wimbledon, London, England, 1970

Vera Brittain was one of the outstanding female poets of World War I. She served as a nurse in a hospital on the **Western Front**.

DID YOU KNOW?
Brittain's book *Testament of Youth*, about her wartime experiences, was adapted for television in 1979. It has since been made into a movie.

Vera Brittain was the daughter of a wealthy paper mill owner.[55] She dreamed of being a writer from an early age. When war was declared, she had been accepted at the University of Oxford, but she decided to become a nurse instead. Most of her fellow students, as well as her brother and her fiancé, had **enlisted**, and Brittain felt she couldn't stay at home. She joined the Voluntary Aid Detachment (VAD), which was set up to assist professional nurses in the event of a war. She trained first at Buxton and then in London.

In 1916, Brittain was posted to a hospital in Malta, and in August 1917, she was sent to the military hospital at Étaples in France, close to the **Western Front**. In her first month at Étaples, nearly 35,000 wounded soldiers were admitted to the hospital—an average of more than 1,000 a day.

The hospital admitted anyone, no matter which side they were fighting on, so at first she worked in the German ward. It was while Brittain was looking after enemy soldiers that she began to realize that the war was not a simple question of right against wrong. It was a much deeper tragedy of human suffering.

Brittain had other reasons to grieve: in 1915, her fiancé Roland Leighton was killed; then, in 1918, her brother Edward was killed. She also lost several other close friends. It was this tragedy, both personal and universal, that inspired Brittain's writing.

TESTAMENT OF YOUTH

Brittain's early poetry recorded what she saw on the wards. *Verses of a VAD* was published just before the end of the war. She dedicated the book to her late fiancé, Roland Leighton.

After the war, Brittain returned to England and continued working as a nurse before attending the University of Oxford starting in 1919. After graduating, she moved to London and started writing fiction. In 1933, nearly 20 years after the war, she wrote the first volume of her autobiography. *Testament of Youth* detailed her experiences as a nurse. It became a global best-seller, and Brittain had a successful career that lasted until her death in 1970. She continued to campaign for the cause that was closest to her heart: **pacifism**.

"When I think of [my brother] Edward in one part of France working to annihilate these very same people that I in another part am working to save, I begin to realize the folly and tragedy of war in a way I never did before."

Vera Brittain on nursing German **casualties**, from a 1917 article[56]

LINK
Read more about Vera Brittain's life and work at **www.biographyonline.net/poets/vera-brittain.html**

This is the manuscript of "Perhaps," Vera Brittain's moving farewell to her fiancé, who was killed in 1915.

Perhaps —
(To R.A.L. Died of wounds in France, December 1915.)

Perhaps some day the sun will shine again,
And I shall see that still the skies are blue,
And feel once more I do not live in vain,
Although bereft of You.

Perhaps the golden meadows at my feet
Will make the sunny hours of Spring seem gay,
And I shall find the white May blossoms sweet,
Though You have passed away.

Perhaps the summer woods will shimmer bright,
And crimson roses once again be fair,
And autumn harvest fields a rich delight,
Although You are not there.

Perhaps some day I shall not shrink in pain
To watch the passing of the dying year,
And listen to the Christmas songs again,
Although You cannot hear.

But though kind Time may many joys renew,

"LOVE AMIDST WAR"

Brittain's early poetry was written from the point of view of a young woman watching her brother, fiancé, and male friends going off to fight. She was still, by her own admission, under the influence of Rupert Brooke, and she saw something **romantic** and heroic about the beginning of the conflict.[57] The reality of war hit her quickly and hard. In 1916, she wrote the moving "Perhaps." It was a painful farewell to her dead fiancé. "Perhaps some day the sun will shine again," she writes.

The tone of Brittain's poetry changed when she started nursing at Étaples. First, her poems were composed quickly during rare moments of rest. She sent them back to her family without much polishing.

Second, Brittain was writing about the real consequences of war, and her personal reactions to it. "Never…have I seen such dreadful wounds," she wrote in 1917.[58] "It gives one a chance to live up to our Motto 'Inter arma caritas.'" This was the Red Cross motto ("Love amidst war"). Brittain used it as the subtitle for her first great poem, "The German Ward," which she wrote at Étaples. "The German Ward" is a completely different poem from anything she had written before. She reports on conditions in the ward—"the bitter groans and laboured breath…and sights and smells of blood and wounds and death." It was as simple and harrowing as Owen's work of the same period.

REMEMBERING THE DEAD

In June 1918, Brittain wrote "To My Brother" to commemorate her brother Edward's bravery at the **Battle of the Somme** in 1916. She wrote: "Your battle-wounds are scars upon my heart, / Received when in that grand and tragic '**show**' / You played your part / Two years ago." Brittain sent the poem to Edward, then serving in Italy—but it arrived too late. He was killed in action just four days after she wrote it.

She returned to the subject of Edward's death, and that of Roland Leighton, time and time again, struggling to deal with the many losses she suffered in a few short years.

DISCUSSION TOPIC

Female war poet
Vera Brittain was one of the few female poets whose poetry of World War I became well known. Are there any qualities to her work that make it different than the poetry of male writers?

LINK
Read more of Vera Brittain's poems at the First World War Digital Poetry Archive: www.oucs.ox.ac.uk/ww1lit/collections/brittain

"After seeing some of the dreadful things I have to see here, I feel I shall never be the same person again, and wonder if, when the war does end, I shall have forgotten how to laugh."

Letter from Vera Brittain to Roland Leighton (1915)[59]

CHARLES SORLEY

Born: Aberdeen,
Scotland, 1895
Died: Loos, France, 1915

Charles Sorley was only
20 years old when he died
in the trenches, but many
consider him to be one
of the most talented
war poets.

DID YOU KNOW?
Sorley was one of the
few poets who expressed
serious sympathy with
the German enemy.

Charles Hamilton Sorley was the son of a college professor who moved the family from Aberdeen, Scotland, to Cambridge, England, when Charles was five.[60] Charles started writing in his teens, submitting poems to the school magazine. He also played soccer, and his favorite pastime was running in the countryside. His love of the natural world and history are qualities that stand out in his early work.

After leaving school, Sorley spent a few months traveling around Europe before starting college. A trip to Germany, where he stayed for just over seven months, was the turning point in his life. He loved every minute of the trip—and he particularly loved the German people. "I felt I was a German," he wrote in February 1914, "and proud to be a German... I felt that perhaps I could die for Deutschland—and I have never had an inkling of that feeling about England, and never shall."[61]

WAR ARRIVES

Blissfully unaware of the gathering storm, Sorley set off on a walking tour of the Moselle Valley in July. On August 2, a couple of days before Great Britain declared war on Germany, he and his friend were arrested as English spies. They spent a night in prison before returning, hurriedly, to England. Sorley applied for a **commission** to become an officer, and within a few days he was accepted as a second lieutenant.

Even then, he was uncertain about the rights and wrongs of the war. "I regard the war as one between sisters," he wrote in a letter of October 1914, "the efficient and intolerant against the casual and sympathetic."[62]

> "Germany's only fault...is a lack of real insight and sympathy with those who differ from her. We are not fighting a bully, but a **bigot**."
>
> Letter from Charles Sorley to his friend A. J. Hopkinson (1914)[63]

Early death

By the time Sorley's battalion was sent to France in May 1915, his attitude toward the war was hardening. A quick encounter with death, when one of his men accidentally blew himself up with a bomb, made Sorley realize the confusion and mess of the fight.

In August 1915, he was promoted to the rank of captain and his leave was canceled. At the outbreak of the Battle of Loos on the **Western Front**, he led his company to the front line, where he was killed by a **sniper**'s bullet in the trenches. He was only 20 years old.

LINK

Find out more about Sorley's life and work at www.firstworldwar.com/poetsandprose/sorley.htm

"YOU ARE BLIND LIKE US"

Sorley only wrote 37 complete poems before he died.[64] But his talent was so great that Robert Graves considered him to be "one of the three poets of importance killed during the war," the other two being Wilfred Owen and Isaac Rosenberg.[65]

What makes Sorley special is his balanced attitude toward the rights and wrongs of World War I. His life in Germany just before the war made him sympathetic to his European neighbors. He also had little faith in Britain's moral rightness—he joined up, he said, "in a spirit of dutiful but unenthusiastic **patriotism**." From the start, he saw the war as a total tragedy rather than a simple battle between good and evil. In one of his most famous poems, "To Germany," written in 1914, he says, "In each other's dearest ways we stand, / And hiss and hate. And the blind fight the blind."

"You are blind like us. Your hurt no man designed,
And no man claimed the conquest of your land.
But gropers both through fields of thought confined
We stumble and we do not understand."

"To Germany" (1914)

British troops advance to attack through a cloud of **poison gas**, as viewed from the trench that they have just left. This remarkable snapshot was taken by a British soldier on the opening day of the Battle of Loos, September 25, 1915.

The final poem

Sorley's two most famous poems take very different attitudes toward the war. "All the Hills and Vales Along" was written at about the same time as "To Germany." Like Brooke's "The Soldier," it is about young men marching off to battle. But unlike Brooke, who saw glory in the coming danger, Sorley saw only death. "All the hills and vales along / Earth is bursting into song, / And the singers are the chaps / Who are going to die perhaps." The only comfort for Sorley, that great lover of nature and history, is that death would reunite men with the earth.

Sorley's poems questioned the popular view of the Germans as cruel monsters, as depicted here in a wartime cartoon "The Gentle German."

Sorley's last poem was found among his belongings after he died and sent home to his parents with his other possessions.[66] It must have been hard for them to read: "When you see millions of the mouthless dead / Give them not praise. For, deaf, how should they know / It is not curses heaped on each gashed head?" Perhaps this is the poem that gives us the best idea of what Sorley might have been capable of if he had lived.

DISCUSSION TOPIC

A sympathetic attitude
Sorley believed that both Great Britain and Germany were wrong to go to war. How does his attitude differ from that of other poets? Did it affect his work?

LINK
Read more about Sorley's work at **www.poemhunter.com/charles-hamilton-sorley**

ALAN SEEGER

Born: New York, New York, United States, 1888
Died: Belloy-en-Santerre, France, 1916

Alan Seeger was an American citizen living in Paris in 1914. He volunteered for the French Foreign Legion and fought for France.

DID YOU KNOW?
His nephew, Pete Seeger, is a famous singer-songwriter.

Alan Seeger grew up in New York and Mexico. He attended Harvard University, where he was friends with the poet T. S. Eliot. He then spent some years drifting between the United States and France, trying to become a writer. In 1912, he moved to Paris. He loved the city and wrote a great deal of very enthusiastic verse about it, but none of it compares to his later work.

When war was declared in August 1914, Seeger could easily have returned home—the United States didn't enter the war until 1917, so there was no need for him to fight. But out of solidarity with his French friends, he volunteered for the French Foreign Legion, which is made up of people from foreign countries who want to fight for France. He went straight into training in Toulouse, France.

Soon Seeger was in the trenches, where he spent the winter of 1914 and much of 1915. The experience was a stark contrast to the noble impulse that inspired him to **enlist** in the first place. "You must not be anxious about my not coming back," he wrote to his mother in June 1915. "The chances are about ten to one that I will. But if I should not, you must be proud... I could not have done otherwise than I did, and I think I could not have done better. Death is nothing terrible after all."[67]

> "Whether I am on the winning or losing side is not the point with me: it is being on the side where my sympathies lie that matters, and I am ready to see it through to the end."

Letter from Alan Seeger to his mother, July 3, 1915[68]

LINK

Find out more about Alan Seeger at www.english.emory.edu/LostPoets/Seeger.html

FIGHTING FOR FRANCE

After many months of active service, including the Battle of Champagne, Seeger's regiment was taken off the front line. The poet spent some time in the hospital, recovering from his battle experiences. In May 1916, he returned to the Somme, and in July he was involved in fighting around the French village of Belloy-en-Santerre. Seeger was among the first line of soldiers sent in to clear German troops from the village, and he was wounded by German machine gun fire. As he lay dying, Seeger was heard cheering on the second wave of advance, which was successful in capturing Belloy.

Seeger's poetry was published in 1917, but it was not successful at the time. Over the years, however, his work has become extremely popular. Seeger is among the foreign soldiers honored by a monument at the Place des États-Unis (United States Place) in Paris.

"THAT RARE PRIVILEGE OF DYING WELL"

Seeger, like Rupert Brooke, died relatively early in the war, before disillusionment with the slaughter had set in. His poetry celebrates the excitement and glory of war, not the brutality and **carnage**. His first war poems expressed the **idealistic** views that made him enlist with the Foreign Legion. He wrote: "I found for all dear things I forfeited / A recompense... More than dull Peace or its poor votaries could, / Taught us the dignity of being men."[69]

Even after Seeger had seen action in the trenches, particularly at the Battle of Champagne, he was obsessed with war as a glorious opportunity. He continued to see a good, early death as preferable to a long, dull life. He best summed up his feelings in his poem "Ode in Memory of the American Volunteers Fallen for France":

"France, to you they rendered thanks
(Seeing they came for honor, not for gain),
Who, opening to them your glorious ranks,
Gave them that grand occasion to excel,
That chance to live the life most free from stain
And that rare privilege of dying well."

Seeger died just before this sentiment of fighting for honor fell out of favor. By the time his poems were published in 1917, attitudes toward the war had changed completely, and he was quickly forgotten. His old college friend T. S. Eliot reviewed Seeger's book *Poems* in 1917. He said "Seeger was serious about his work... It is high-flown, heavily decorated and solemn. Alan Seeger...lived his whole life on this plane."[70]

DISCUSSION TOPIC

The "American Rupert Brooke"?

Robert Graves called Seeger an "American Rupert Brooke."[71] Is this a fair comparison? What are the main differences between Seeger and Brooke?

LINK

Read Seeger's poetry at www.poemhunter.com/alan-seeger

Seeger's reputation

Since then, Seeger has become more famous in death than he ever was in life. The poem "I Have a Rendezvous with Death" was a favorite of President John F. Kennedy's, and it has become a fixture in anthologies of American poetry. [72] Like all Seeger's poetry, it is a highly **romantic** approach to the subject. It is far removed from the realism of Graves, Sassoon, and Owen. For Seeger, death will come in spring, "when apple-blossoms fill the air...at midnight in some flaming town... I shall not fail that rendezvous." These were the words of a man who still believed that death in battle was glorious, and who regarded war as "the majesty of strife."[73] He died still believing in these ideals.

> "If it must be, let it come in the heat of action. Why flinch? It is by far the noblest form in which death can come. It is in a sense almost a privilege."
>
> Letter from Alan Seeger to *The New York Sun*, May 22, 1915[74]

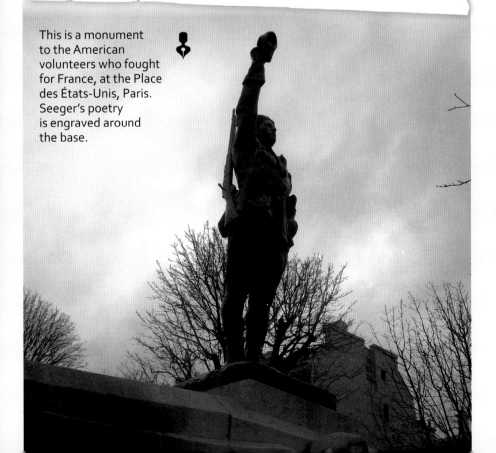

This is a monument to the American volunteers who fought for France, at the Place des États-Unis, Paris. Seeger's poetry is engraved around the base.

OTHER VOICES

Hundreds of poets from many countries wrote about World War I. Some of them became famous, while some wrote only a couple of significant works. Some survived the war, but many died in the trenches. Their work, and their life stories, give us great insight into the events of 1914 to 1918—not just from the point of view of the **Allies**, but also from the "enemy," Germany.

EDMOND ADAM (1889-1918)

Edmond Adam was a civil engineer who volunteered for active service in 1914. He fought right through the war until his death in August 1918. Very little is known of Adam's life, but he started contributing poems to the antiwar magazine *Les Humbles* in 1918. This included his best-known work "Coqs de Combat," which shocked with its direct, violent language.

TRY READING: "Coqs de Combat" (or "Gamecocks")

LAURENCE BINYON (1869-1943)

Englishman Laurence Binyon was too old to **enlist** as a soldier, but he volunteered as a hospital orderly in France, tending to the wounded from Verdun. After the war, he resumed his job at the British Museum in London, where he became an internationally famous art expert. His poem "For the Fallen," written in 1914 after the Battle of the Marne, has become one of the most famous war poems of all time.

TRY READING: "For the Fallen"

EDMUND BLUNDEN (1896-1974)

Edmund Blunden was **commissioned** as an English officer in 1915 at the age of just 19. He survived two solid years at the front, including at Ypres and the Somme, without serious physical injury. He wrote a great deal of poetry during and after the war. His poems were not as graphic as those of his friend Siegfried Sassoon, but they often dealt with the **psychological** effects of the experience in a profound and moving way.

TRY READING: "1916 Seen from 1921"

MARGARET POSTGATE COLE (1893–1980)

At the beginning of the war, Margaret Cole's brother was imprisoned in England as a **conscientious objector**. This inspired her to campaign against conscription (forcing people by law to join the army) and for **pacifism**. Her war poems express her outrage at the violence of the war and the waste of young men's lives. After the war, Cole wrote a lot about history and politics. She also wrote many detective novels with her husband, George Cole.

TRY READING: "The Veteran"

IVOR GURNEY (1890–1937)

A gifted composer, Ivor Gurney was studying at the Royal College of Music in London when war was declared. He enlisted in 1915 and wrote a good deal of poetry while serving in France. In 1917, he was wounded and gassed in France. He returned to England to recover. After the war, Gurney suffered a serious breakdown and spent much of the rest of his life in psychiatric hospitals. He continued to write poetry and music.

TRY READING: "Strange Hells"

ERNEST HEMINGWAY (1899–1961)

American Ernest Hemingway (right) is remembered today as one of the most famous novelists of the 20th century. At the age of 18, in 1918, he spent two months driving ambulances on the Italian front, before being badly wounded by shrapnel and sent to the hospital. He remembered his wartime experiences in poems that were written in the 1920s, as he was starting his career as a writer.

TRY READING: "Killed Piave— July 8—1918"

RUDYARD KIPLING (1865-1936)

Rudyard Kipling was already one of Britain's most famous writers when war was declared. (He wrote *The Jungle Book* in 1894.) Being too old to fight himself, he encouraged his son John to enlist. In 1915, John was killed at the Battle of Loos, at age 18. Kipling was overwhelmed by grief and guilt, which he expressed in his poetry. It is a rare poetic response to the war from a bereaved parent.

TRY READING: "My Boy Jack"

ARCHIBALD MacLEISH (1892-1982)

American Archibald MacLeish was a student at Harvard Law School when the United States entered the war. He served as an ambulance driver and later in the artillery at the second Battle of the Marne. He started writing poetry during the war, which he survived. His brother, Kenneth, did not. Some of his best poetry is about his brother's death. After the war, MacLeish rose to the office of librarian of Congress, assistant secretary of state, and cofounder of the United Nations Educational, Scientific, and Cultural Organization (UNESCO).

TRY READING: "The Silent Slain"

BENJAMIN PÉRET (1899-1959)

Frenchman Benjamin Péret served with the French army in the Balkans and Greece. He started writing poetry during this time. After the war, Péret became one of the leading poets of antiwar artistic movements in France. He published his first volume of poetry in 1921. He later fought in the Spanish Civil War and immigrated to Mexico.

TRY READING: "Petite Chanson des Mutilés" (or "Little Song of the Maimed")

HERBERT READ (1893-1968)

Herbert Read was a student at the University of Leeds in England when war was declared. He served in France, received the **Military Cross** and the Distinguished Service Order, and reached the rank of captain. Most of his war poetry was published in his second book, *Naked Warriors* (1919). After the war, Read became an art critic and a supporter of anarchism, where individuals enjoy freedom without government.

TRY READING: "Meditation of a Dying German Officer"

EDWARD THOMAS (1878–1917)

Edward Thomas (right) was already an established poet in Great Britain when the war started. He was celebrated for his portraits of nature and traditional landscapes, especially in his famous poem "Adlestrop." Despite his age and his young family, Thomas enlisted in 1915. He arrived in France as a second lieutenant in 1917 but was killed shortly afterward, at the Battle of Arras. His war poetry is remarkable for its focus on the natural world.

TRY READING: "In Memoriam (Easter 1915)"

ERNST STADLER (1883–1914)

Born in Alsace-Lorraine, now part of Germany, Ernst Stadler studied for a while at England's University of Oxford before returning home and becoming a poet. He was influenced by the philosopher Friedrich Nietzsche, and he believed war was a necessary crisis to renew Europe. He went off to fight in 1914 full of hope and excitement. He was killed by a British grenade a few weeks later.

TRY READING: "Der Aufbruch" (or "Setting Out")

AUGUST STRAMM (1874–1915)

August Stramm was a central figure in the circle of Berlin artists known as the Expressionists. Today, he is best known as a playwright. His poetry, like his plays, is tense, violent, and **fragmented**. It captures some of the fear and panic as well as the excitement that greeted the outbreak of war in Germany. Stramm served as an officer in France and on the Eastern Front, where he died in hand-to-hand combat.

TRY READING: "Wunde" (or "Wound")

TIMELINE

World War I was a global war centered in Europe. It began on July 28, 1914, and lasted until November 11, 1918. At the time, it was known as the Great War, but then became known as World War I after there had been a second world war, from 1939 to 1945.

1914: OPENING MOVES

WAR DECLARED
HOPES OF QUICK RESULTS FADE—STALEMATE AND TRENCH WARFARE

June 28	Archduke Ferdinand of Austria is assassinated in Sarajevo by Serbian nationalist Gavrilo Princip
July 28	Austria-Hungary declares war on Serbia
August 1	Outbreak of war: Germany declares war on Russia
August 3	Germany declares war on France
August 4	Germany invades Belgium. Great Britain declares war on Germany. President Woodrow Wilson declares U.S. **neutrality**.
August 26	Start of the Battle of Tannenberg, Germany's biggest success of the war on the Eastern Front (which was in Russia)
September 5	Start of the first Battle of the Marne, which halted the German advance into France and resulted in a stalemate and trench warfare
October 14	Start of the first Battle of Ypres, an attempt by both sides to bring the war to a swift conclusion. After weeks of fighting in Belgium and huge losses, neither side had gained the advantage.
October 29	Turkey enters the war
October 30	Poet Ernst Stadler dies
December 21	First German air raid on Britain
December 25	Unofficial Christmas truce is declared by troops on the **Western Front**

1915: STALEMATE IN THE TRENCHES

ALLIES FAIL TO STOP GERMAN ADVANCES ON WESTERN FRONT—GERMANS ALSO SUCCESSFUL IN EAST—MASSACRE AT GALLIPOLI

February 4	German **U-boat** attacks ships in an attempt to cut off supplies to Britain
February 19	Beginning of **Allied** land and sea action on the **Dardanelles** and **Gallipoli**, Turkey, which results in the Turkish siege of Allied forces
April 4	Rupert Brooke's "The Soldier" is read out loud in St. Paul's Cathedral in London
April 22	Start of the second Battle of Ypres with the first use of **poison gas** by Germans
April 23	Poet Rupert Brooke dies
April 25	Allied landings at Gallipoli
May 7	Sinking of British passenger liner *Lusitania* by a German U-boat off the Irish coast, with several American **casualties**. The event threatens U.S. neutrality.
September 1	Poet August Stramm dies
September 25	Opening of the second Battle of Champagne, an unsuccessful French attempt to halt the German invasion. This sets the scene for the 1916 Battle of Verdun.
October 13	Poet Charles Sorley dies
December 19	Field Marshal Douglas Haig becomes commander-in-chief of the troops that were sent to the Western Front
December 28	Withdrawal of Allied troops from Gallipoli begins

MASSIVE BATTLES AT SOMME AND VERDUN KILL HUNDREDS OF THOUSANDS

No Decisive Victory in France—Biggest Ever Naval Battle at Jutland

Publication of Robert Graves's first volume of war poetry, *Over the Brazier*

February 21	Start of the Battle of Verdun, as Germany attempts to secure a stranglehold on France. This leads to the longest battle of the war.
April 27	Lord Kitchener, British secretary of state for war, asks for military assistance from the United States, which is still neutral
May 31–June 1	Battle of Jutland, the biggest naval battle in history, off the coast of Denmark: 14 British and 11 German ships are sunk, with no decisive outcome
July 1	Start of the **Battle of the Somme**. The British Army suffers nearly 60,000 casualties on the first day.
July 4	Poet Alan Seeger dies
September	Publication of *Soldier Poets: Songs of the Fighting Men*, an influential anthology of war poetry that sells well in the United States
September 15	First use of tanks by the British, on the Somme battlefield
November 18	End of the Battle of the Somme, with small advances made by the Allies
November 28	First German airplane raid on London

U-BOAT CAMPAIGN BRINGS U.S. INTO THE WAR

Russian Revolution—Deadlock on Western Front

Publication of Graves's *Fairies and Fusiliers*

January 9	Germany launches a policy of unrestricted U-boat warfare
February	Strikes and protests mark the start of the **Russian Revolution**
February 3	The United States severs relations with Germany
February 23	Germany makes a tactical withdrawal to defensible positions on the Hindenburg Line in northeastern France
March 15	Tsar Nicholas II of Russia abdicates
April 6	The United States declares war on Germany
April 9	Start of the Nivelle Offensive, another unsuccessful French attempt to repel German invasion, with costly battles at Aisne and Champagne. Poet Edward Thomas dies.
May	Publication of Siegfried Sassoon's first collection of war poetry, *The Old Huntsman*
June 26	First U.S. troops arrive in France
July 6	T. E. Lawrence (known as Lawrence of Arabia) captures territory from the Turks in the Arab Revolt
July 16	Passchendaele offensive begins in Flanders, an Allied attempt to push the Germans out of Belgium
July 30	Sassoon's "Finished with the War" is read to members of the UK government
July 31	Major British offensive at third Battle of Ypres
August	Wilfred Owen and Sassoon meet in Craiglockhart War Hospital, Edinburgh, Scotland
August 4	Vera Brittain starts work at Étaples Hospital on the Western Front
September 1	Riga Offensive marks further German success on the Eastern Front
November 7	Start of "October Revolution" marks a decisive phase of Russian Revolution and beginning of the Russian Civil War, as Vladimir Lenin takes control
November 20	British launch a surprise attack at Cambrai in France, breaking through the Hindenburg Line

GERMAN SPRING OFFENSIVE NEARLY DEFEATS ALLIES
ALLIED COUNTER-ATTACK TURNS THE TABLES
HINDENBURG LINE BREACHED—ARMISTICE

January	Russia leaves the war
March 21	Germany launches the **Spring Offensive**, the first of five assaults against the Allied forces, starting with the Battle of Picardy, taking back much of the Somme. The fighting now becomes more fluid, not tied to the front lines that had existed for the previous three years.
April 1	Poet Isaac Rosenberg dies
April 9	Germans launch the second phase of their offensive at Battle of the Lys, leading to significant gains in Flanders and the near collapse of the Allied armies in Europe
May 25	German U-boats appear in U.S. waters
May 27	Third phase of German offensive begins at the third Battle of the Aisne
June 9	Opening of the fourth phase of German offensive (Battle of the Matz)
July	Publication of Sassoon's *Counter-Attack*
July 15	Final phase of the German offensive (second Battle of the Marne) leads to German defeat and a decisive turning of tide in favor of the Allies
July 16–17	Murder of Tsar Nicholas II and his family in Russia
July 18	Start of Allied counterattack, seizing strategical initiative from the Germans
August 8	Start of Battle of Amiens marks the beginning of the Allied "Hundred Days Offensive," forcing German troops back to the Hindenburg Line
August 24	Poet Edmond Adam dies
September 27	First major breaches of the Hindenburg Line by the Allied forces
October 3–4	Germans and Austrians send notes to U.S. President Woodrow Wilson requesting an **armistice**
October 8	Start of decisive Battle of Cambrai leads to a speedy Allied victory
October 21	Germany calls off its U-boat campaign
October 30	Turkey agrees to armistice with Allies
November 3	German navy mutinies at Kiel
November 4	Poet Wilfred Owen dies
November 7	Germany enters armistice negotiations
November 9	Kaiser Wilhelm II abdicates
November 11	Armistice goes into effect as fighting ceases at 11 a.m.

PEACE CONFERENCE
—THE TREATY OF VERSAILLES

January 10	Start of communist revolt in Berlin
January 18	Peace negotiations open in Paris
January 25	Peace conference accepts principle of a League of Nations
June 21	German fleet scuttled (sinks itself) at Scapa Flow
June 28	Treaty of Versailles is signed in the Hall of Mirrors at Versailles, in France

Find Out More

World War I has been inspiring artists, writers, and filmmakers for 100 years. Poetry is one of the most important ways in which we can find out about what it was like to live through the war, but here are some other suggestions.

NONFICTION BOOKS

Barber, Nicola. *World War I* (Living Through). Chicago: Heinemann Library, 2012.
How did the war affect people's everyday lives? Find out more in this survey of battles in Europe and life on the home front.

Brittain, Vera, and friends. *Letters from a Lost Generation*. Boston: Northeastern University Press, 1999.
The correspondence between Brittain, her brother, her fiancé, and her friends gives an intimate picture of what it was like for young people during the war.

Worth, Richard. *America in World War I* (Wars That Changed American History). Milwaukee: World Almanac Library, 2007.
Learn more about the role the United States played in World War I. This book includes primary sources and many photographs.

NOVELS

A Farewell to Arms, Ernest Hemingway: The great American novelist used his own experience of serving in Italy during World War I to create a powerful story of the relationship between an American soldier and a British nurse.

All Quiet on the Western Front, Erich-Maria Remarque: One of the classic war novels, written in 1929 by a German veteran, it tells the story of life in the trenches. It has been filmed twice, in 1930 and 1979.

War Horse, Michael Morpurgo: This is the story of Joey, a horse sent to serve on the Western Front, and the attempts of his owner, Albert, to get him home alive. It was made into a successful play and then a movie, which was directed by Steven Spielberg.

PLAYS

Going Up, Louis Hirsch, Otto Harbach, and James Montgomery: This 1917 Broadway musical tells the story of a writer who serves as a pilot in World War I and uses his flying skills to win the attention of a girl he loves.

Journey's End, R. C. Sherriff: First performed in London in 1928, Sherriff's play has become one of the most famous depictions of life in the trenches.

My Boy Jack, David Haig: This play is based on the true story of the famous writer Rudyard Kipling, who lost his son in World War I.

What Price Glory?, Maxwell Anderson and Laurence Stallings: This Broadway play captured the way soldiers really spoke to each other during the war.

GLOSSARY

Allies, Allied Powers Great Britain, France, Russia, Italy (from 1915), and the United States (from 1917), the group of countries that fought against the Central Powers (Germany, Austria-Hungary, the Ottoman Empire under Turkish rule, and Bulgaria) in World War I. Other nations were also involved on both sides.

armistice truce. An armistice was signed between the Allies and Germany to cease all fighting on the Western Front during World War I. It took effect on November 11 at 11 a.m.—the "eleventh hour of the eleventh day of the eleventh month" of 1918.

bantam small but tough variety of poultry; also used to describe people who are small in stature

Battle of the Somme one of the bloodiest battles of the war. It claimed hundreds of thousands of casualties for an overall Allied advance of 5 miles (8 kilometers). It lasted over five months, from July 1 to November 18, 1916.

bigot person who insists on believing in one set of ideas despite any evidence to the contrary

British Empire countries ruled by Great Britain from the 17th to the 20th century. By 1914, it was the biggest empire the world had ever seen.

carnage mass slaughter

casualty wounded or injured person

commissioned given official command over people in lower ranks in the army, air force, or navy

conscientious objector someone who refuses to fight because he or she believes that war is wrong. Conscientious objectors during World War I were regarded as cowards and usually sent to prison.

contemporary person living at the same time as someone else, usually roughly the same age

court martial trial held by an army, navy, or air force to decide whether someone has broken military law. To be court-martialed is to be sent to trial.

Dardanelles long, narrow strip of sea in Turkey. It is important because it allows ships to get from the Mediterranean to the Black Sea. It was the scene of one of the most important battles of World War I.

enlist sign up or volunteer to join the army, navy, or air force

fragment small part of something, like an exploding shell. It is also used to describe a small section of a poem, sometimes an unfinished work.

Gallipoli peninsula on the western shore of the Dardanelles

idealistic believing more in ideals than reality. The idealistic approach to the war stressed duty, honor, and glory rather than death and injury.

Jewish immigrant Jewish person who leaves his or her home country to settle in another country

Military Cross one of the highest awards for bravery in the British Army

neutrality not fighting for either side in a war. The United States was neutral in World War I until 1917.

no-man's-land area of land between two opposing armies that is not controlled by either army

over the top when soldiers came out of their trenches and started advancing toward the enemy over exposed ground, usually under heavy fire

pacifism belief that war is always wrong, and that peace should be maintained at any price

patriotism deep and unquestioning love of one's country, and a willingness to do anything for it

poison gas type of chemical weapon. Poison gases were supposed to be illegal, but they were frequently used by both sides in World War I. Mustard gas and chlorine gas were two of the most common. They burn the skin, lungs, and eyes, often with fatal results.

preface introduction—for example, to a collection of poetry—in which the author says a few words about what he or she is trying to achieve

psychoanalysis way of helping people with mental or emotional problems, encouraging patients to talk about their fears as a way of understanding them. The method was still regarded as quite new during World War I.

psychological relating to the mental and emotional state of a person

romantic in literature, something that expresses a belief in ideals, courage, and beauty. It is not just relating to love or relationships.

Russian Revolution series of political upheavals in 1917 that turned Russia from a royal society under the rule of the tsar to a Soviet Republic

satire, satirical form of writing or other expression that uses humor to expose stupidity or evil

shell shock aftereffects of trench warfare, with its constant danger, explosions, and death. It caused many soldiers to experience terrible nightmares and depression. It was also known as neurasthenia. Today, we call it post-traumatic stress disorder.

show slang term used by soldiers for a battle

sniper gunman, often located at some distance from his or her target, relying on good aim

Spring Offensive series of military campaigns staged in 1918 by the Germans, who were trying to win the war in France

U-boat German submarine, used to devastating effect on Allied shipping; from the German *Unterseeboot* (literally, "undersea boat")

Western Front major war zone in northeast France and Belgium. It marked the boundary between invading German forces who were pushing west, and the Allied forces who were trying to push them back.

Notes on Sources

1 Tim Cross (ed.), *The Lost Voices of World War I* (Bloomsbury, 1988), p. 37
2 www.demographia.com/db-uspop1900.htm
3 www.census.gov/population/www/popclockus.html
4 demog.berkeley.edu/~andrew/1918/figure2.html
5 esa.un.org/wpp/Documentation/pdf/WPP2010_Highlights.pdf
6 www.infoplease.com/ipa/A0104673.html
7 www.economist.com/node/15174418
8 usa.usembassy.de/etexts/his/e_prices1.htm
9 money.cnn.com/2012/09/12/news/economy/median-income-poverty/index.html
10 Biographical details from Dominic Hibberd (ed.), *Wilfred Owen: War Poems and Others* (Chatto & Windus, 1973)
11 Ibid., p. 59
12 Ibid.
13 Ibid., p. 68
14 Ibid., pp. 61–62
15 Ibid., p. 101
16 Letter to Leslie Gunston, August 22, 1917, in Hibberd, *Wilfred Owen*, p. 73
17 Jean Moorcroft Wilson, "The Hermit of Heytesbury," www.guardian.co.uk/books/2003/mar/29/featuresreviews.guardianreview28
18 "I was one with Wilfred Owen, though on a lower plane of poetic expression," ibid.
19 Biographical details from Rupert Hart-Davis, *Oxford Dictionary of National Biography* (*DNB*), www.oxforddnb.com/view/article/35953
20 Ibid.
21 Ibid.
22 www.guardian.co.uk/world/2008/nov/10/first-world-war-siegfried-sassoon
23 Siegfried Sassoon, *Memoirs of an Infantry Officer* (Faber, 1930)
24 Hart-Davis, *DNB*
25 Letter to Susan Owen, in Hibberd, *Wilfred Owen*, p. 101
26 Sassoon's comments on the origins of his poetry are included in Rupert Hart-Davis (ed.), *Siegfried Sassoon: The War Poems* (Faber, 1983)
27 Ibid., p. 57
28 Biographical details from Ian Parsons (ed.), *The Collected Works of Isaac Rosenberg* (Chatto & Windus, 1979)
29 Ibid., p. xxii
30 Ibid., p. xxiv
31 Ibid., p. 259
32 Ibid., p. ix
33 Ibid., p. xvii
34 Ibid., p. xvii
35 Ibid., p. ix
36 Ibid., p. 219
37 Figures from BBC, www.bbc.co.uk/history/worldwars/wwone/battle_somme.shtml

38 Parsons, *Isaac Rosenberg*, p. ix

39 Ibid., p. 248

40 Ibid., p. 27

41 Ibid., p. 146

42 Ibid., p. 149

43 Ibid., p. 151

44 ibid., p. 170

45 Ibid., pp. 169–170

46 www.rupertbrookeonskyros.com/Intro.htm

47 The First World War Poetry Digital Archive, www.oucs.ox.ac.uk/ww1lit/education/tutorials/intro/brooke/vsoldier.html

48 Ibid., www.oucs.ox.ac.uk/ww1lit/collections/graves

49 Biographical details from www.robertgraves.org

50 "*Good-Bye to All That* by Robert Graves," projects.oucs.ox.ac.uk/jtap/rose/goodbye.html

51 www.robertgraves.org/trust/index.php?id=2

52 en.wikipedia.org/wiki/Robert_Graves#cite_note-8

53 Michael Pharand, "Avoiding the Psychoanalytic Confession-Box: Robert Graves and W. H. R. Rivers," *Gravesiana*, www.robertgraves.org/issues/17/8133_article_387.pdf

54 Robert Graves, *Poems About War* (Cassell, 1988), p. 10

55 Biographical details from Vera Brittain, *Because You Died: Poetry and Prose of World War I and After* (ed. Mark Bostridge, Virago, 2008)

56 Ibid., p. 103

57 Ibid., p. 124

58 Ibid., p. 219

59 www.spartacus.schoolnet.co.uk/Jbrittain.htm

60 Biographical details from Hilda D. Spear (ed.), *The Poems and Selected Letters of Charles Hamilton Sorley* (Blackness Press, 1978)

61 Letter to the Master of Marlborough, February 20, 1914, in Spear, *Charles Hamilton Sorley*, p. 87

62 Letter to A. J. Hopkinson, October 1914, in Spear, *Charles Hamilton Sorley*, p. 94

63 Ibid.

64 www.spartacus.schoolnet.co.uk/FWWsorley.htm

65 Spear, *Charles Hamilton Sorley*, p. 9

66 Ibid., p. 26

67 William Archer, introduction to "Poems by Alan Seeger," www.gutenberg.org/cache/epub/617/pg617.html

68 Ibid.

69 From "The Aisne"

70 Cross, *Lost Voices*, p. 34

71 Graves, *Poems about War*, p. 10

72 answers.google.com/answers/threadview/id/779825.html

73 From "The Aisne"

74 Cross, *Lost Voices*, p. 3

Biographical details for "Other Voices" (pp. 52–55) from *Chambers Biographical Dictionary*, *The Penguin Book of First World War Poetry* (ed. Jon Silkin, Penguin, 1979), and Cross, *Lost Voices*

INDEX

Adam, Edmond 52
"All the Hills and Vales Along" (Sorley) 47
American volunteers 48–51
"Anthem for Doomed Youth" (Owen) 14, 15
"Attack" (Sassoon) 21

Bantam Battalion 22, 26
Binyon, Laurence 27, 52
Bloomsbury Group 29
Blunden, Edmund 52
Boer Wars 9
"Break of Day in the Trenches" (Rosenberg) 5, 25
British Empire 8
Brittain, Vera 40–43
Brooke, Rupert 5, 23, 28–33, 38, 42, 47

Cambridge Apostles 29
casualties 26, 27, 30, 32
cemeteries 12, 27
Churchill, Winston 29, 31
Civil War 9
Cole, Margaret Postgate 53
conscientious objectors 11, 53
Cornford, Frances 29
"Counter-Attack" (Sassoon) 5, 21
court-martial 17, 37
Craiglockhart War Hospital 12, 17, 37, 57

Dardanelles 30
"Dead Boche, A" (Graves) 38
"Dead Man's Dump" (Rosenberg) 25
disillusionment 17, 19, 38, 45, 50
"Dulce et Decorum est" (Owen) 5, 15

Eliot, T. S. 48, 50

"Everyone Sang" (Sassoon) 21

"For the Fallen" (Binyon) 52
French Foreign Legion 48

Gallipoli 16, 30, 32
gas attacks 6, 15, 37, 46
German poets 55
"German Ward, The" 43
Good-Bye to All That (Graves) 35, 36
Graves, Robert 5, 20, 34–39, 46, 50
Gurney, Ivor 53

Hemingway, Ernest 5, 53

"I Have a Rendezvous with Death" (Seeger) 51

Jews 22, 24, 25, 26

Kipling, Rudyard 54

language, direct and powerful 20, 24, 38, 43, 52
Ledwidge, Francis 6
Loos, Battle of 45, 46, 54

MacLeish, Archibald 54
Marsh, Edward 20, 23
memorials 5, 31, 49, 51
military hospitals 36, 40–41

natural world 44, 47, 55
"Next War, The" (Graves) 38

"Ode in Memory of the American Volunteers Fallen for France" (Seeger) 50
"Old Vicarage, Grantchester, The" (Brooke) 33
"outsider" status 25, 34
Owen, Wilfred 5, 10–15, 20, 35, 38, 46

pacifism 21, 22, 33, 53
patriotism 15, 29, 32, 36, 46
Péret, Benjamin 54
"Perhaps" (Brittain) 42
psychological effects of war 7, 17, 37, 52, 53

Read, Herbert 54
Rivers, W. H. R. 37
romantic idealism 14, 32, 33, 38, 42, 47, 50, 51
Rosenberg, Isaac 5, 22–27, 46
Russian Revolution 8

Sassoon, Siegfried 5, 11, 12, 13, 14, 15, 16–21, 23, 24, 25, 35, 37, 38
Seeger, Alan 4, 5, 48–51
shell shock 7, 12, 17, 37
"Soldier, The" (Brooke) 28, 31, 32, 33
Somme, Battle of the 19, 20, 26, 27, 35, 43, 49
Sorley, Charles 5, 7, 44–47
Spring Offensive 13, 27
Stadler, Ernst 55
Stramm, August 55

Testament of Youth (Brittain) 7, 40, 41
Thomas, Edward 55
"To Germany" (Sorley) 46
"To My Brother" (Brittain) 43
trench warfare 7, 11, 21, 36

Western Front 7, 32, 40, 45
"When I'm Killed" (Graves) 39
women poets 29, 40–43, 53